JOHN CENA

by Michael Sandler

Consultant: Eric Cohen
Professional Wrestling Guide for About.com
prowrestling.about.com

BEARPORT
PUBLISHING

New York, New York

Credits

Cover and Title Page, © Ethan Miller/Getty Images; TOC, © George Napolitano/FilmMagic/Getty Images; 4, © Matt Roberts/ZUMA Press/Newscom; 5, © Moses Robinson/Getty Images; 6, © Moses Robinson/Getty Images; 7, © AP Photo/Rick Scuteri; 9A, Courtesy of Fletcher6/Wikipedia; 9B, © Peter Gray; 9C, © courtyardpix/Shutterstock; 10L, © Lucas Dawson/Getty Images; 10R, Courtesy of Springfield College; 11, © Hulton Archive/Getty Images; 12, © Nils Jorgensen/Rex USA/BEImages; 13, © EuroStyle Graphics/Alamy; 14, © Titan Sports/Everett/Rex USA/BEImages; 15L, © Carrie Devorah/WENN.com/Newscom; 15R, © Matt Roberts/ZUMA Press/Newscom; 16L, © Bob Levey/Wire Image/Getty Images; 16R, © Carrie Devorah/WENN.com/Newscom; 17, © KMazur/WireImage/Getty Images; 18, © Milan Ryba/Globe Photos/ZUMA Press/Newscom; 19TL, © Don Arnold/WireImage/Getty Images; 19BL, © Ethan Miller/Getty Images; 19R, © imago sportfotodienst/Newscom; 20L, © WWE FILMS/Album/Newscom; 20R, © 20thCentFox/Courtesy Everett Collection; 21, © Ethan Miller/Getty Images; 22T, © AP Photo/Rick Scuteri; 22B, © Ethan Miller/Getty Images.

Publisher: Kenn Goin
Senior Editor: Lisa Wiseman
Creative Director: Spencer Brinker
Photo Researcher: We Research Pictures, LLC
Design: Debrah Kasier

Library of Congress Cataloging-in-Publication Data

Sandler, Michael, 1965–
 John Cena / by Michael Sandler.
   p. cm. — (Wrestling's tough guys)
 Includes bibliographical references and index.
 ISBN 978-1-61772-573-9 (library binding) — ISBN 1-61772-573-0 (library binding)
 1. Cena, John. 2. Wrestlers—United States—Biography—Juvenile literature. I. Title.
 GV1196.C46S26 2012
 796.812092—dc23
 [B]

                              2012003325

For more information, write to Bearport Publishing Company, Inc., 45 West 21st Street, Suite 3B, New York, New York 10010. Printed in the United States of America.

10 9 8 7 6 5 4 3 2 1

Contents

Let's Go, Cena!

John Cena had come a long way. As a young wrestler in 2001, he competed in tiny gyms where nobody knew his name. Now, ten years later, he was standing in a huge arena. Thousands of fans were chanting, "Let's go, Cena!"

John Cena in the ring before a match in 2009

By 2011, John had held the **WWE Championship** nine times. Another win would give him a record tenth championship!

John was already excited even before the crowd began cheering for him. The WWE Championship was at stake. John had once held it, but now it belonged to his **opponent**, Alberto Del Rio. John was determined to win the **title** back.

Early in the match, however, John struggled. Alberto pounded him with kicks to the ribs and chest. Would John be able to turn the match around?

Alberto (shown here) and John's match took place as part of the WWE's Night of Champions in Buffalo, New York, on September 18, 2011.

The Tenth Title

In the ring, John never gave up. Using all the strength in his 6-foot-1 (1.85-m), 251-pound (114-kg) body, he took control of the match. He hammered Alberto with powerful **shoulder blocks** and unleashed a deadly **leg drop**. He also showed off the powerbomb—lifting Alberto above his head and dropping him to the canvas.

John performing a leg drop

Finally, he locked Alberto up in the unbreakable STF—Stepover Toehold Facelock. Alberto had no choice—he **tapped out**. The match was over, and for a record tenth time, John Cena was the WWE Champion!

John holds up the WWE Championship belt.

In an STF, John traps one of the other wrestler's legs between his own. Then, pressing down on his opponent's back, John locks both his arms around his opponent's head.

The Skinny Kid

When John was growing up in West Newbury, Massachusetts, people would never have guessed that he would one day become a wrestler. As a kid, John was really, really skinny. He didn't look like a tough guy. Neighborhood kids often gave him a hard time. They picked on John because of his size and because he seemed different. He didn't dress like everyone else and liked hip-hop instead of rock music. Sometimes bigger kids would try to beat him up.

Finally, John had enough. "To protect myself," remembers John, "I started lifting weights."

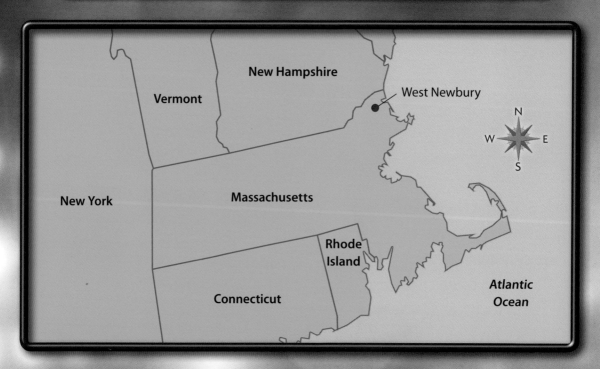

John was born on April 23, 1977, in
West Newbury, Massachusetts.

West Newbury is a town in Massachusetts that is home to more than 4,000 people.

John played football in high school at Cushing Academy.

When John first started lifting weights in seventh grade, he worked out every day on a weight bench his dad had bought him. Soon after, he started going to a gym to lift weights for an even better workout.

Becoming Strong

As John continued lifting weights, he grew bigger and stronger. Soon he was no longer a skinny kid. By age 16, John was packing 215 pounds (98 kg) of muscle. He worked out all the time. He even continued his workouts after graduating from high school and attending Springfield College in Massachusetts.

Over the years, John has spent countless hours in the gym, getting into the best shape possible.

After graduating from high school, John attended Springfield College in Massachusetts.

John used his size and strength to play **center** for the Springfield College Pride football team. A skilled player, he was even named to an **All-American** team.

In college, John studied exercise physiology (*fizz*-ee-OHL-oh-jee), which is the study of how the body works. Doing so taught him how to make his body even stronger. As he studied and exercised, his passion for weightlifting slowly turned into a dream. He wanted to become a champion **bodybuilder**.

Bodybuilders spend many hours a day training. Former bodybuilder Arnold Schwarzenegger (shown here) used to train for four to six hours a day.

Discovering Wrestling

After graduating from college in the late 1990s, John decided to head to Venice Beach, California, where many of the best bodybuilders trained. One day, while working out in a Venice gym, he met a student from a wrestling school called Ultimate Pro Wrestling. As a kid, John had always liked wrestling. The classes the student told John about sounded exciting. John decided to give them a try.

Venice, California, is famous for bodybuilding on the beach.

John quickly discovered that he not only enjoyed being in the ring but was good at the sport, too. About one year later, WWE **talent scouts** spotted John wrestling at the school. Impressed with his strength and wrestling ability, they asked him to join the WWE.

In 2001, the WWE sent John to a school in Louisville, Kentucky, to improve his wrestling skills. There, he had his first wrestling matches as part of Ohio Valley Wrestling.

Hulk Hogan (shown here) is one of John's childhood wrestling heroes.

The Big Time

By 2002, John was ready for his first televised WWE match. John wrestled hard, but his more experienced opponent, Kurt Angle, **pinned** him for the win. John wasn't discouraged. He knew this was just the beginning!

Kurt Angle (left) in action in 2005

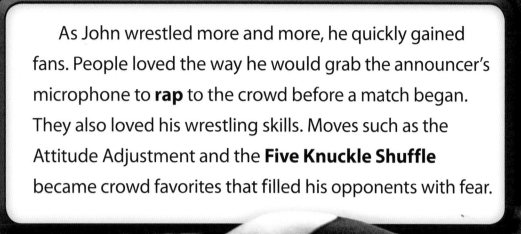

As John wrestled more and more, he quickly gained fans. People loved the way he would grab the announcer's microphone to **rap** to the crowd before a match began. They also loved his wrestling skills. Moves such as the Attitude Adjustment and the **Five Knuckle Shuffle** became crowd favorites that filled his opponents with fear.

John with the microphone during a match in 2009

John performs the Attitude Adjustment on fellow wrestler Big Show.

The Attitude Adjustment is one of the moves that John likes to use to finish a match. To perform this move, he lifts his opponent onto his shoulders behind his head, and then flips him down onto the mat.

15

A Big Match

About two years into his WWE career, John got a chance to wrestle for a title. At 7 feet (2.1 m) tall and more than 450 pounds (204 kg), his opponent, Big Show, looked more like a mountain than a man. Though John was 6 feet 1 (1.85 m) and weighed more than 240 pounds (109 kg), Big Show made him look tiny.

Still, John had no fear. He attacked Big Show with tornado-like force, wearing out his giant **foe**. To finish the match, John lifted Big Show high overhead and tossed him to the mat. Then he jumped on top of Big Show for the pin.

Big Show

John lifting Big Show over his head

John's win over Big Show at WrestleMania XX (20) in March 2004 earned him the WWE's United States Championship.

John shows off his WWE United States Championship belt after defeating Big Show at WrestleMania XX (20).

Title After Title

In 2005, John set his eyes on an even bigger prize, the WWE Championship. To earn it, he had to beat the fiery JBL—John Bradshaw Layfield—at WrestleMania 21. JBL controlled much of the match, but in the end, John beat his foe, finishing him off with the savage Attitude Adjustment. The skinny kid from Massachusetts was now the world's greatest wrestler.

John prepares to slam JBL during WrestleMania 21.

In ten turns as champion, John has held the title for more than a thousand days.

In the WWE, no one holds a title for long. John, however, seemed to keep it for longer than anyone else, quickly winning it back if he lost it in a match. The list of wrestlers he's defeated to keep the title includes wrestling's very best: Triple H, Edge, Randy Orton, Batista, and The Miz. Keeping the title belt away from John is impossible!

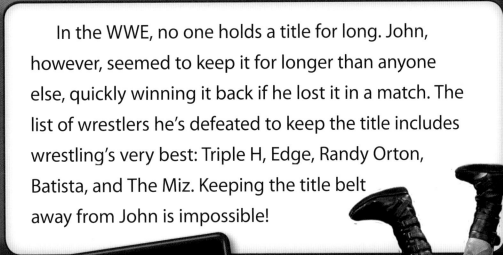

John (left) slams fellow wrestler Batista during a 2010 match.

John (left) puts Edge into a headlock during a 2006 match.

John (standing) picks up Randy Orton during a match in 2009.

Wrestling Forever

Today, John is not only a huge wrestling star but also a big entertainment star. Still a hip-hop fan, he recorded a hit rap album in 2005 called *You Can't See Me*. He's appeared in television shows and movies, such as *The Marine* (2006) and *Legendary* (2010). There's almost nothing, it seems, that John can't do.

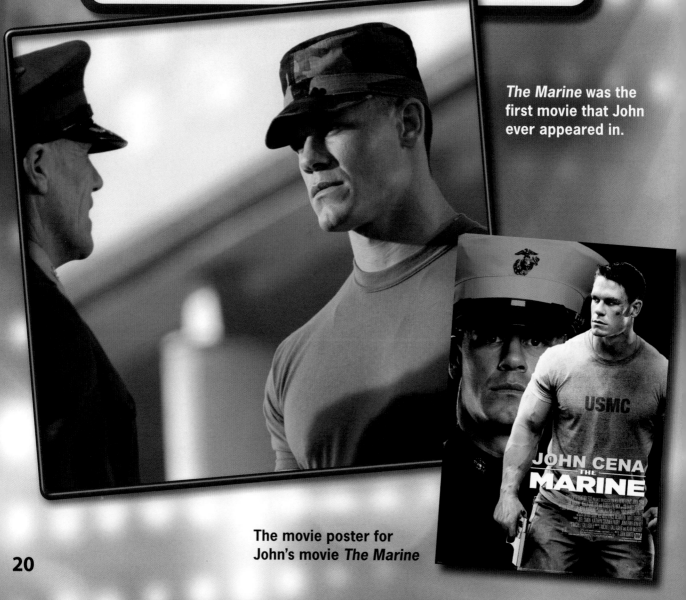

The Marine was the first movie that John ever appeared in.

The movie poster for John's movie *The Marine*

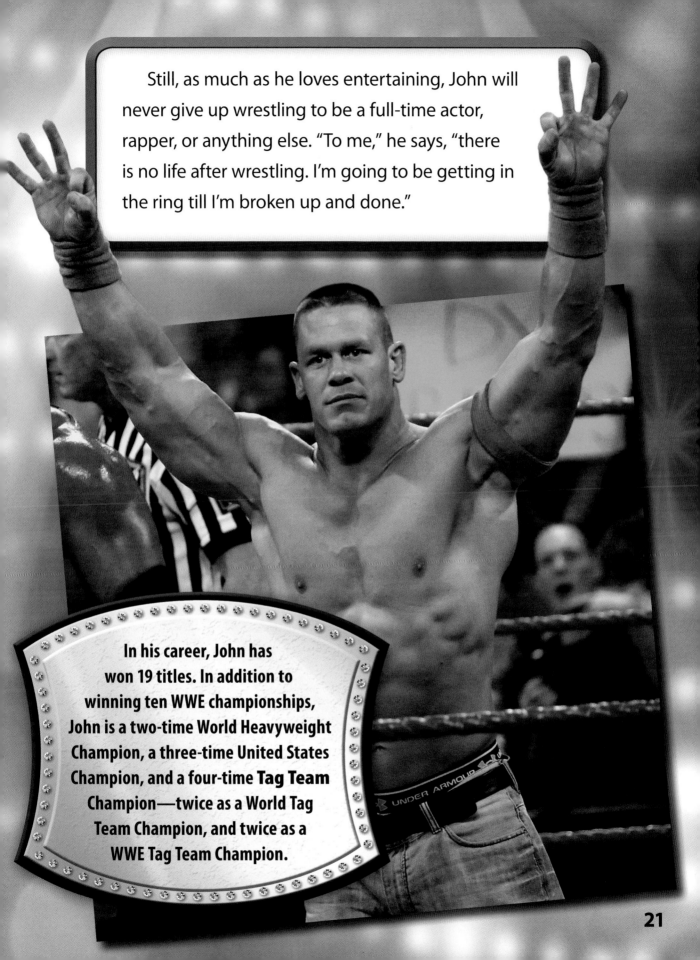

Still, as much as he loves entertaining, John will never give up wrestling to be a full-time actor, rapper, or anything else. "To me," he says, "there is no life after wrestling. I'm going to be getting in the ring till I'm broken up and done."

In his career, John has won 19 titles. In addition to winning ten WWE championships, John is a two-time World Heavyweight Champion, a three-time United States Champion, and a four-time **Tag Team Champion**—twice as a World Tag Team Champion, and twice as a WWE Tag Team Champion.

The John Cena File

Stats:

Born:	West Newbury, Massachusetts
Height:	6' 1" (1.85 m)
Weight:	251 pounds (114 kg)
Greatest moves:	STF, Attitude Adjustment, Five Knuckle Shuffle

Fun Facts:

- In seventh grade, John weighed just 125 pounds (57 kg).

- When he's not wrestling, John likes to barbecue and play chess.

- Only three wrestlers—Bob Backlund, Hulk Hogan, and Bruno Sammartino—have held the WWE Championship longer than John.

John after performing an Attitude Adjustment on Randy Orton

Glossary

All-American (*awl*-uh-MER-uh-kuhn) a high school or college athlete who is named one of the best at his or her position in the entire country

bodybuilder (BOD-ee-*bild*-ur) a person who builds his or her body through diet and exercise and competes in competitions against others to see who has the best-developed body

center (SEN-tur) an offensive position on a football team; a center begins each football play by snapping the ball to the quarterback

Five Knuckle Shuffle (FIVE NUHK-uhl SHUHF-uhl) a wrestling move made popular by John Cena in which John bounces off the ropes before dropping onto his opponent and hitting him with his fist

foe (FOH) an enemy

leg drop (LEG DROP) a move in which a wrestler jumps into the air and drops his or her leg onto a part of an opponent's body

opponent (uh-POH-nuhnt) an athlete or team that another athlete or team competes against in a sporting event

pinned (PIND) ended a match by holding an opponent's shoulders down on the floor for a count of three

rap (RAP) to perform a song in which the words are spoken rather than sung

shoulder blocks (SHOHL-dur BLOKS) when a wrestler strikes an opponent with his or her shoulder

tag team (TAG TEEM) a wrestling event in which teams of wrestlers battle each other; usually only one wrestler from each team is allowed in the ring at a time, and teammates switch places inside and outside the ring by "tagging" or hand-slapping each other

talent scouts (TAL-uhnt SKOUTS) people who have the job of finding talented athletes for a team, group, or league

tapped out (TAPT OUT) when a wrestler has tapped on the floor to let the referee know that he or she is giving up

title (TYE-tuhl) a championship

WWE (DUHB-*uhl*-yoo-DUHB-*uhl*-yoo-FF) the main pro wrestling organization in the United States

WWE Championship (DUHB-*uhl*-yoo-DUHB-*uhl*-yoo-EE CHAM-pee-uhn-*ship*) one of the WWE's most important titles, along with the World Heavyweight Championship

Bibliography

Eck, Kevin. "WWE Champ Is a Triple Threat." *The Baltimore Sun* (October 14, 2006).

"John Cena Interview." *Men's Fitness* (April 2005).

Millado, Nate. "Unchained JC Cena." *Men's Fitness* (April 2009).

WWE.com

Read More

Black, Jake. *The Ultimate Guide to WWE*. New York: Grosset & Dunlap (2011).

Shields, Brian. *WWE John Cena*. New York: DK (2009).

Stone, Adam. *John Cena*. Minneapolis, MN: Bellwether Media (2012).

Learn More Online

To learn more about John Cena, visit
www.bearportpublishing.com/WrestlingsToughGuys

Index